Cecily

A play for women

Gillian Plowman

Samuel French - London
New York - Toronto - Hollywood

ISBN 0 573 13227 5

Please see page iv for further copyright information.

CECILY

First presented by Runneymede Drama Group at the QE 2 Theatre, Woking, on 6th October, 1990, with the following cast:

Sheila	Judith Dolley
Ellen, her sister	Frankie Godliman
Cecily, her daughter	Claire Dolley

Directed by Colin Dolley
Designed by Paul Marshall
Lighting by Malcolm Meades

The action takes place in Sheila's and Cecily's home

Time—the present and the very recent past

COPYRIGHT INFORMATION

(See also page ii)

Other plays by Gillian Plowman
published by Samuel French

David's Birthday
The Janna Years
Me and My Friend
Tippers
Two Summers

CECILY

The living-room of Sheila's and Cecily's home

The room is colourful, with exercise balls, cubes and paper flowers. There is a coloured quilt and a rubber exercise mat on the floor

Cecily is dozing in a wheelchair. Sheila is also on stage. In her forties and casually dressed, her mood is black. She picks up the quilt and throws it over Cecily, then takes it off and folds it. She lies down and stretches on the exercise mat

Ellen enters. She is also in her forties but elegantly dressed, wearing a pair of high heels. She looks at Cecily

Ellen She's always asleep.

Sheila She's not always asleep.

Ellen When I come in, she is.

Sheila We've been extremely busy doing exercises—over the balls, around the cubes, lie flat, this leg, that leg ... there's no improvement and I'm worn out.

Ellen I'll stay with her for a bit. You got something to do?

Sheila I've got something to do for the next twenty years. (*She groans as she rises into a sitting position*)

Ellen If you want anything from the shops, I can bring it on my way in tomorrow.

Sheila Another ten boxes of incontinence pads.

Ellen I can't manage ten at once.

Sheila Bring five then.

Ellen How long will they last?

Sheila Till Sunday. Then the shops will be closed.

Ellen I'll manage six.

Sheila I never used disposable nappies.

Ellen I don't know why you didn't.

Sheila Because ...

Ellen Because ...

Sheila Because, because, because, because, because ...

Ellen I would have ...

Sheila Then you ... should have ...

Ellen It's lunch time.
Sheila Wake her up then.

Ellen shakes Cecily

Ellen Cecily, it's Ellen. Wake up.

Cecily wakes and stares directly at Ellen

Cecily 'Lo. 'Len.
Ellen Hallo, Ellen.
Cecily 'Lo. 'Len.
Sheila It's difficult for anybody. Stupid name.
Ellen Have it back then.
Sheila If I'd liked it in the first place, I wouldn't have swapped it with you.

Cecily falls asleep again. Sheila shakes her. They make sure that Cecily stays awake during this conversation

Talk to her. Tell her about the names.
Ellen We swapped names, you see, Cecily, your mother and I.
Sheila Our parents, who were very cruel and unkind to us ...
Ellen No they weren't ...
Sheila They made us move to that God forsaken place with that God-awful school ...
Ellen They couldn't really help it ...
Sheila We told them we hated it.
Ellen It was father's job. Your grandfather, Cecily.
Sheila And they didn't care.
Ellen We didn't like the new school.
Sheila We hated it. All those moon-faced children staring. You'd think they'd never had new girls before.
Ellen The teacher's name was Miss Brierly. She was very tall.
Sheila And she smelt. You should be extremely careful about personal hygiene, Cecily, when you're working with children who only come up to your waist.
Ellen We were in the same class to start with ...
Sheila And Miss Brierly said "Hallo, Sheila," and you said ...
Ellen I'm not Sheila, I'm Ellen.
Sheila (*as Miss Brierly*) But I'm sure your mother said ...
Ellen That's Sheila.
Cecily Sheila, Sheila.

Ellen (*as Miss Brierly*) Surely you're Ellen?
Sheila I'm Sheila.
Ellen (*as Miss Brierly*) Are you sure you're not Ellen?
Sheila I ought to know who I am, miss.
Ellen I didn't know you didn't like "Ellen" though.
Sheila It didn't suit me. It suits you. Ellen. Elegant.
Ellen I wonder if you'd have been elegant if you'd have kept it.

Pause

Sheila With a kid you become something else.
Ellen It's funny. We couldn't tell her that before, could we?
Sheila We can tell her anything now.
Ellen She's gone to sleep again.

Sheila slaps Cecily's face

Don't do that.
Sheila She's supposed to be awake. She shouldn't really sleep more than ten hours a day. It's bad for her.

Ellen takes Cecily's hands and talks to her again, picking up the different coloured objects as she mentions the colours

Ellen We swapped clothes. All the time. I bought red things and yellow things, and your mother bought blue things and green things and we swapped them all about.
Sheila We swapped bicycles.
Ellen Boy friends.
Sheila I was pretty serious about Simon Toms, too.
Ellen Why did you swap him then?
Sheila To see how serious he was.
Ellen Boys were pretty stupid in those days, Cecily. If one sister gave them the brush-off, and the other was there with tea and sympathy, they were an absolute push-over.
Sheila It didn't matter about the others.
Ellen I didn't know it mattered about him.

Pause

Sheila We swapped jobs once or twice.
Ellen I chose the advertising one especially. I knew it would suit you. "I'm awfully sorry to give you so little notice, but my sister

is an excellent secretary, has super references and I can bring her in tomorrow. . . ." Anything to save them hassle!

Sheila Yes, I liked that one. Brought out the artist in me.

Ellen I hated your newspaper one.

Sheila You were promoted within the first six months.

Ellen Slept with the boss.

Sheila Oh God, I might have known.

Ellen Men are disgusting, promoting you because you sleep with them.

Sheila (*looking at Ellen*) That was the difference between us, Cecily. Sex. I didn't and she did. I wanted to be a virgin when I married. Whilst your Aunt Ellen . . .

Ellen What?

Sheila . . . wanted the experience.

Cecily yawns

Ellen Do we know about Cecily? Are you a virgin, Cecily?

Cecily No.

Sheila Yes you are.

Cecily No.

Sheila Well you will be from now on. Time for a walk, Cecily. Come on. Walk.

Sheila pulls Cecily into a standing position in front of the wheelchair

Cecily Want to go bed.

Sheila You're going for a walk first. The doctor said. Ellen!

Ellen takes Cecily's other arm and they walk her round the room. She drags her legs

Ellen She's a lazy thing, isn't she?

Sheila She's naughty. Smack her bottom.

Ellen I don't believe in smacking children.

Sheila smacks Cecily who yelps and walks better for a minute

Cecily (*singing to the tune from* The Wizard of Oz) Because, because, because, because, because . . .

Ellen is uncomfortable in her high heels and kicks them off. Cecily sneezes and wipes her nose on the front of Ellen's blouse

Ellen Cecily! Oh Christ, Sheila, this blouse has to be dry-cleaned.

Ellen leaves them to get a tissue from her bag. Sheila lets Cecily slide to the floor

Sheila She's given me a bad back, you know.
Ellen Put her in the wheelchair. I'll take her for a ride.

Sheila puts the wheelchair beside Cecily and goes out

Cecily cannot get into the chair on her own. Ellen struggles to help her. When she is seated, Cecily strokes Ellen's hair and smiles at her. Ellen kisses Cecily. Cecily touches Ellen's mouth and smears her lipstick. Ellen tissues her mouth clean and combs her hair

Why, Cecily? Why did you ever want to go on the back of that wretched motor bike?
Cecily Because, because ...
Ellen Shhh. (*She pushes Cecily round the room*) Don't go to sleep.

Ellen stops the wheelchair and goes to the front to look at Cecily who is pulling her hair down in front of her face

Don't hide your face. It's a pretty face. You've got pretty hair. (*She combs Cecily's hair and puts a coloured scarf in it. She puts some lipstick on her*) That was the trouble really. You were too pretty. Had too many boyfriends. Like me. But why did you have to choose that idiot with the motor bike?
Cecily Michael.
Ellen Yes, Michael. Do you remember him, Cecily?
Cecily Michael ... Michael ... (*She starts to moan*)
Ellen It's all right. He just wasn't very good at riding his motor bike.
Cecily Michael!
Ellen Did you sleep with Michael, Cecily?
Cecily Dead.
Ellen You know that, do you? You know he's dead?

Cecily screams and bites Ellen's face, digging her nails into her shoulders. Ellen cries out in pain and pushes Cecily back into the chair

Sheila enters

Sheila Difficult?
Cecily Fuck, fuck, fuck, fuck ...

Sheila She's trying to annoy you. What did you do to upset her?
Ellen You shouldn't bite people, you know.
Cecily Fuck!
Ellen Stop it! Stop it! You don't use words like that. It's not nice. Why does she do that?
Sheila Expressive dysphasia. Sometimes, when she's angry, it's all she can say.
Ellen It's disgusting!
Sheila It has a certain ring to it. Isn't that right, Cecily?
Ellen You don't let her get away with it, do you?
Cecily Bed!
Sheila We're going to have lunch first. Ellen's come to lunch.
Ellen Why don't you let her go to bed?
Sheila Because that's the easy way out.

Pause

And I do it. I put her to bed and let her sleep and then I have some peace. I put two pads on her and leave her there. She dreams. I don't know what she dreams about but she's happy when she's asleep. She laughs.

Pause

And I leave her there.
Ellen I can't stay to lunch.
Sheila Sod off then.
Ellen It's you, isn't it? That's why she's like she is—all this filthy language. What's the matter with you?
Sheila First you say you've come to lunch. Then you haven't. Then you have, then you haven't . . . If you don't stay, we won't have any.
Ellen Why not?
Sheila Can't be bothered.
Ellen Won't she want to eat?

Sheila shrugs

You need a break, don't you? They can arrange it. They've got people, nice people, who can look after her whilst you have a holiday.
Sheila I don't want a holiday.

Ellen Come away with Gary and me for a bit. You won't have to do anything.

Sheila Why can't SHE come away with Gary and you?

Ellen I wouldn't mind, you know that. It's Gary. He doesn't know what to do with her.

Sheila I don't know what to do with her. I don't want her any more.

Ellen What?

Sheila You heard what I said.

Ellen You don't mean it.

Sheila I don't know what to do with her.

Ellen They'll help you.

Sheila Who?

Ellen The doctors, social workers . . .

Sheila How?

Ellen She goes to the day centre . . .

Sheila And the rest of the time, I don't know what to do with her.

Ellen You'll get used to it. It's early days yet. She'll get better . . . I mean, she'll improve, won't she?

Sheila She won't improve.

Ellen You're strong, Sheila. You're just going through a bad patch. You love her.

Sheila I love her, yes, I love her. I love her, I love her but I don't know what to do with her . . . (*She breaks down*)

Cecily cries

Ellen Shh. Go to sleep, Cecily. Go to sleep, there's a good girl.

Cecily goes to sleep almost straight away

Sheila I dream, you know. Cecily has an accident—motor-bike crash and she's brain-damaged. Permanently, the doctors say. She'll be like a tiny child with no control over her body. I pray to God and promise everything I have and more—my life—if it could only be the day before the accident. When I wake up, it is the day before, and she's her normal self, and the tears are pouring down my face because I'm so happy, you've no idea. Only it's still the dream, and I wake for real and the accident has happened . . . I have to keep on living through it, keep on . . . living through it . . .

Ellen Do you want me to get some lunch?

Sheila Yes please.
Ellen What?

Sheila looks at her

Is she still a vegetarian?
Sheila No.
Ellen Why not?
Sheila It doesn't matter now, does it?
Ellen It does. Her principles still matter.
Sheila Principles belong to a clear, undamaged brain. They are the conclusion of logical thought. Cecily doesn't think any more.
Ellen We ought to respect her views, that's all.
Sheila She doesn't have any views.
Ellen You don't know that. They're there, somewhere. Cecily, what would you like to eat?
Cecily Fuck!
Ellen Stop it!
Cecily Fuck, fuck, fuck ... (*She screams*)

Sheila pushes Cecily out

The Lights change for a flashback sequence. Ellen has arrived at the house and gets a book out of her bag, reading the title

Ellen Simple vegetarian meals.

There are voices outside and Sheila and Cecily (as she was before the accident) talk as they enter

Sheila I don't see why you can't be careful—just check your pockets before you put things out for the wash.
Cecily Oh Mum, it's boring. Boring chores ...
Sheila It's boring having no clean clothes. That's a bent two p. That could have rogered the drum. That could have cost a fortune ...
Cecily But it didn't roger the drum and it didn't cost a fortune ...
Sheila I can't afford it.
Cecily Michael would have done it. He's good with mechanical things. Hi, Ellen.
Sheila So why didn't he?
Cecily 'Cos you didn't tell me the machine was broken.
Sheila Because you weren't here. Just check your pockets, that's all I ask because I don't see why I should do it!

Cecily To make sure that two p's don't go into the machine.

Sheila Just help me, won't you?

Cecily I'm sorry. I'm a lousy turn-out for all the years you've put into me, aren't I?

Sheila Oh, Cecily!

They hug each other

Cecily Talking of bent things, how's Gary?

Ellen Missing you. He sent you this. He approves.

Cecily Is he going vegetarian too?

Ellen No, but he approves of anyone who is.

Sheila I don't think she'll get enough protein.

Ellen He says you haven't been over lately.

Cecily Been busy.

Ellen Studying?

Cecily Everything in the whole wide world.

Ellen You're in love.

Sheila He's a bad influence.

Cecily He's stunning.

Ellen It had to happen. Gary will be upset. He thinks you're in love with him.

Cecily Well of course I am. But this is different. Michael's got incredible sex appeal.

Ellen He'll be even more upset.

Sheila He takes up too much of her time. She's got exams . . .

Cecily I study, I study. He keeps up my morale. His family are very rich.

Ellen Case proven.

Sheila They've disowned him.

Ellen Why?

Sheila He's a hooligan.

Cecily He burned his mother's fur coat. He's a bit of an activist. Animal rights, nuclear waste. He's always doing something outside the South African Embassy. He hates his family being rich. He told them. His father burned all of Michael's things after the fur coat episode and told him to go into the world naked and make his own way.

Sheila Which he does, on a motor-bike.

Ellen Naked?

Cecily He does quick despatches.

Sheila He roars away from here pretty quickly at two o'clock in the morning. It has got to stop.
Cecily Do you mean he'd better stay all night?
Sheila People are complaining.
Cecily About the noise?
Sheila Of course about the noise.
Ellen Fair comment, I would say.
Cecily And I agree.
Sheila Oh good!
Cecily He'd better stay all night?
Sheila It's immoral. And distracting.
Ellen Which is worse?
Cecily Ridiculous discussions about bent two p pieces are distracting.
Sheila Do you want to wash your clothes by hand then?
Cecily Mum, that doesn't matter. The exams matter, because that's my future. Michael matters because he keeps my soul warm. The washing machine doesn't matter. It's temporary. Dirty clothes are temporary.
Sheila They're permanent if nobody washes them.
Cecily I just want you to understand, that's all.
Sheila And I want you to . . . do the washing!

Sheila exits

Cecily Is she going through the menopause or something?
Ellen Maybe she's got tired of coping with everything on her own. As you said, Michael gives you moral support.
Cecily She's used to it.
Ellen You take her for granted, Cecily.
Cecily I didn't stop her, you know. She could have got married. I'd have liked a father. It's a hell of a burden on me, being the only person she lives with.

Pause

My father did die, didn't he? He's not still floating around somewhere?
Ellen I never knew him. Sheila was working in London. She never talked about him.
Cecily And she still won't. But I've a right to know.
Ellen You probably know all that there is.

Cecily I intend to track him down one of these days. His family. They'll be surprised.
Ellen You know his name?
Cecily Oh yes. Simon. Simon Toms.

Pause

Ellen What good will it do, Cecily? Tracking down his family? He never knew about you himself.
Cecily Didn't he? Is that what she told you? I thought she never talked about him.
Ellen She told me that much. She was ashamed, Cecily.
Cecily Of me?
Ellen Of the situation. Don't make it bad for her. She loves you.
Cecily I am me, Ellen. However I got here, I'm entitled to be here.
Ellen True.
Cecily And as the man said, I'll do it my way.

Pause

I'll find him.
Ellen Don't.

Pause

Cecily Can you keep a secret?
Ellen Don't tell me anything that will make my relationship with Sheila difficult.
Cecily This won't. Look! (*She pulls her jeans down at the back and shows Ellen her bottom*)
Ellen (*reading*) "Do it today!" Cecily! Will it come off?
Cecily No. It's tattooed on.
Ellen You'll regret it.
Cecily I won't. It'll remind me how I feel now. When I'm young and have energy and can do whatever I want. Life is there for me, but it's all too short. So get stuck in. Do it now, and don't miss it. Actually, you're the only person who's seen it.
Ellen Not even Michael?
Cecily He will do, when the time's right.
Ellen So we're not doing it now?
Cecily Not that, no. We're sharing each other's heads and souls now.
Ellen The time will come.

Cecily Oh yes. And soon. (*She laughs*) Do you think Gary would lend me some cash. We're windsurfing this weekend and it's my turn to pay for the petrol.

Ellen gives her ten pounds

Thanks, Gary. He fancies me, you know. Have you seen that look in his eye? He's a dirty old man, that husband of yours.

Ellen You lead him on.

Cecily I don't.

Ellen And now that I've seen that tattoo on your bottom, I'd really rather you didn't, all right?

They look at each other

Cecily Being fatherless, I had to practise my burgeoning sexuality on somebody. I'm going to play my drums. See ya.

Cecily makes drum noises with her hands and mouth and goes out

The Lights change back to the present

Sheila enters

Sheila What are we having?

Ellen What?

Sheila We'll starve to death then, shall we?

Ellen How is she?

Sheila She's all right. She's on the toilet.

Ellen Do you leave her there?

Sheila What do you want to do? Get lunch or go and wipe her bottom.

Ellen It's this blouse . . .

Sheila Which prevents you doing either. It doesn't matter if you have dirty clothes, you know.

Ellen I've got a meeting this afternoon.

Pause

I brought her a present. (*She gets a carrier bag and produces a brightly coloured manipulative toy*)

Sheila Ellen, the favourite aunt! The one who was able to spoil her!

Ellen I can't do anything right, can I? For heaven's sake, Sheila . . .

Sheila You never had to smack her, did you? Never had to say no. Never had to scrimp and save. Always able to buy her the pretty things that little girls want. Do you know how difficult it was when she came back from holidays with you, with her toenails painted and a tube of lipstick in her bag? Demanding to stay up and watch television till all hours? "Ellen lets me!"
Ellen Holidays aren't normal times.
Sheila Tantrums she had, kicking and biting me. Hating me. I was always the baddie.
Ellen She was a spirited child. I only had holidays. You were lucky, you had all of her.
Sheila You didn't want all of her!
Ellen And you did. You're her mother, Sheila.
Sheila You're her mother, Ellen!

Pause

Cecily (*off*) 'Len!
Sheila So go and wipe her bottom.

They look at each other

Ellen goes out

Sheila God, dear God, why won't you let it be before . . .

The Lights change to before the accident

Cecily enters

Cecily *Was ist los, Muschi?*
Sheila Just thinking.
Cecily What about?
Sheila Cecily, do you . . . you've missed having a father, haven't you?
Cecily A lot of the girls have terrible trouble with their fathers.
Sheila I sometimes feel guilty that you haven't had a proper family life . . .
Cecily Was he good-looking?
Sheila I think so.
Cecily Did you love him very much?
Sheila If I'm honest, I don't really know.
Cecily You're getting vague and elderly, Mother. Do you want to come to a party with me?

Sheila You can't take your mother to a party.
Cecily It's a punk party. We could dress you up so that no-one will recognize you.
Sheila They frighten me, punks.
Cecily They frighten themselves. It's taking the first step. But at least then you have an identity. You are somebody.
Sheila Everybody's somebody.
Cecily Tell that to the kids who sleep on the streets. We've got space, Mum. Two or three beds at least ...
Sheila Don't be silly.
Cecily It's not silly ... it's thinking of others ... and it wouldn't be just you and me then ... it's not silly ... silly ... silly ... silly ...

Cecily's voice fades as she leaves the room

The Lights return to the present

Sheila is crying

Sheila Please let it be before ...

Ellen wheels Cecily in

(*Turning to them*) All right, I'll come to the party, and I'll wear black lipstick and green hair and chains on my hips, and they'll still know who I am. Who am I, Cecily?
Cecily Mummy!
Sheila They'll know, you see, who I am.
Ellen We could have bananas for lunch.

Cecily shouts out happily. Ellen picks up the bananas from the fruit bowl

Sheila rushes out to the kitchen and brings in some more

Sheila We've got millions of bananas.
Ellen Long, thin zippy ones ...
Sheila Short, fat, mushy ones ...
Ellen Hygienic ...
Sheila Nourishing ...
Ellen And yellow!
Sheila If we're going to eat hygienic bananas, we ought to wash our hands.
Ellen I've just washed mine.

Sheila What about Cecily?
Ellen She didn't wipe her bottom, I did.
Sheila She's been doing all sorts of things with her hands.
Ellen That's what hands are for.

She starts to do hand clapping with Cecily, then wipes her hands with wet wipes

Cecily (*singing*) Because, because, because, because, because . . .
Ellen There, that'll do.
Sheila Have a banana, Cecily.
Cecily Thank you.

She manages to peel it. Cecily likes bananas

Ellen She's quite clever, isn't she?
Sheila Cecily Armstrong, B.Sc. She would have been.
Ellen The way she can peel that banana on her own. You're very clever, Cecily.
Cecily Michael likes nanas.
Sheila He doesn't. Not now.
Ellen I don't think we ought to talk about Michael.
Sheila You talk about him, Cecily.
Cecily Mummy not like Michael.
Sheila The more she talks, the better.
Ellen She does like him.
Sheila I don't. Anyway, he's dead.
Ellen Don't, Sheila.
Sheila Michael liked bananas before he was dead.
Ellen Sheila, I'm sure it's not right.
Cecily Fuck, Michael.
Ellen Now, you see, you've started her off.

Cecily starts to shout

What about the drums, Cecily? Do you like to play the drums?
Cecily No, no!
Sheila She can't hold the sticks. They fall out of her hands.

Cecily screams and bangs her head. They wait for her to stop. She then makes the noise of brushes on drums, which she does very well

Ellen What do they say you should talk about?
Sheila They who?

Ellen Don't they advise you?

Sheila They tell you to keep her awake. They don't tell you what to do with her whilst she's awake, apart from keeping her occupied. They don't tell you what to talk about.

Ellen Do you like banana sandwiches, Cecily?

Cecily Yes.

Ellen What other sandwiches do you like?

Cecily Chicken.

Ellen Chicken?

Cecily Yes.

Ellen But you're vegetarian.

Cecily is puzzled

Sheila You don't like the way they keep chickens all cooped up in tiny boxes so they can't even turn around, and spend their whole lives without ever taking a step. Do you, Cecily?

Cecily reaches for the quilt and puts it over her head

Ellen There's a lot of fat in meat. Cholesterol. Especially if you don't take a lot of exercise. Gary has almost given up.

Sheila Meat or exercise?

Ellen He's doing the half-marathon next week. I'll take Cecily to watch. We can go to the finishing post.

Sheila She was going to enter.

Ellen What?

Sheila She was going to surprise Gary. She'd been training. He kept on about it and she was going to show him. I don't think it's a good idea to take her. It might upset her.

Ellen Like feeding her meat?

Sheila It'll make her frustrated and she'll start swearing at everybody. You won't be able to cope.

Pause

Did you see her tattoo?

Ellen What?

Sheila When you wiped her bottom?

Ellen No.

Sheila I'll show it to you.

Ellen I don't want to see it.

Sheila I want you to see it.

She takes the quilt off Cecily and bends her over, pushing her skirt down. Cecily protests

Ellen Leave her alone, Sheila.

Sheila She actually went to a tattooist and had words drilled into her bottom.

Cecily No! No!

Sheila I would never have known, would I? I haven't seen her bottom since she was a little girl. A little girl . . .

She is still trying to show Ellen the tattoo. Cecily is crying

Ellen Just tell me what it says.

Sheila Read it for yourself.

Cecily is yelling

Ellen "Do it today".

Sheila It says "Do it today". You knew?

Ellen I did see it.

Sheila Why did you say you didn't? When? When did you see it?

Ellen I've seen it, that's all.

Sheila When?

Ellen One day. She showed it to me.

Sheila Before?

Ellen Yes.

Cecily cries

Pull her clothes up.

Sheila You pull her bloody clothes up. Why? Why do you always know everything? I'm her mother. I should know.

Ellen I know. I'm sorry.

Cecily Do it today.

Sheila Do it, then! Do it today! Bloody do it!

She shouts into Cecily's face. There is silence

I've got a headache.

Ellen I expect you have. Why don't you go and lie down?

Sheila It's worse this way. Worse than if she'd been killed.

Ellen Whilst there's life, there's hope.

Sheila Michael's parents can remember him as he was. We've got a new Cecily. She needs a new tattoo.

Ellen It might take years, but there's always a chance.
Sheila Delete "Do it today". Add "It might take years".

Pause

Ellen Go and lie down. I'll stay with her.
Sheila What about your meeting?
Ellen I'll ring them.
Sheila I want to swap back again, Ellen. I want my name back. And you can have your daughter back.
Ellen Shall I see the doctor for you? Tell him you can't cope?
Sheila I mean it.
Ellen We said it was forever. That no matter what happened, it was forever.
Sheila Nothing is forever.
Ellen You're tired and you've made yourself ill.
Sheila I don't want her any more. No, that's not true. I want her and I love her . . . so much . . . so much . . . but I do it all wrong. I can't look after her properly. All the time I'm loving her, I'm hating her. And I hit her.
Ellen That's understandable. It's for her own good—to make her do things properly . . .
Sheila I hit her because I hate her. Do you hear that, Cecily?

Cecily puts the quilt over her head

I don't. I don't. I want to be Ellen again. To wear nice clothes and go to work and visit friends. I want to call on my way home and bring Cecily a present, and ask if there's any shopping I can do and then leave. I want to be elegant. And I don't want to hit her any more.
Ellen She'll have to go into a home.
Sheila There aren't any homes she can go into. They're sending people out, not taking them in!
Cecily (*throwing off the quilt*) Hallo.
Ellen Hallo, Cecily.
Cecily What's matter?
Sheila Ellen wants you to go and live in a home.
Cecily 'Len's home?
Ellen No!
Cecily Gary likes me.
Ellen No. He doesn't. He can't bear to see her like this. He won't have her.

Cecily puts the quilt back over her head

Cecily 'Bye.
Sheila I shall tell him.
Ellen What?
Sheila That you're Sheila.
Ellen I told him years ago. He found it quite amusing.
Sheila That we swapped everything?
Ellen Yes.
Sheila That the baby was yours?

Silence

I was the virgin, Gary, she was the one who made the mistake.
Ellen Stop it.
Sheila How sad that you had to go abroad to work. She really pined for you. Missed you so much that she went to bed with our old boy friend, Simon Toms.
Ellen I did miss him. I just needed someone.
Sheila And became pregnant.

The Lights change for a flashback

What are you going to tell Gary?
Ellen Nothing.
Sheila He's bound to find out.
Ellen He's staying in Saudi till the end of the year. He wants to make enough to buy us a really nice house. Sheila . . .

The Lights return to the present

Sheila So we swapped once more, Gary. My virginity for her baby. I became the unmarried mother.
Ellen You wanted her. You were besotted with her.
Sheila She was Simon's child.

Pause

Ellen Gary would never have married me. Not with another man's child. Afterwards, I often thought it would be all right if I told him. He became so fond of Cecily. Well, he's been like a father to her. But I didn't, because she was yours, and we'd said it was forever . . .
Sheila And you were too bloody scared to.
Ellen He said he'd adopt her if anything happened to you.

Sheila Well now something has happened to me.
Ellen Please, please don't tell him.

Cecily makes drum noises from under the quilt

The Lights change to a flashback. Beat music fills the air, disco lights flash on and off and Cecily throws back the quilt and appears in a sequined bolero with drumsticks in her hand as she mimes a drum solo to the sound of music. The noise gets louder, and as the drumming ends, there is recorded applause and cheering as Cecily takes a bow in the spotlight. She is full of energy and punches the air with her fists

Cecily And God created Woman!
Ellen Well done, Cecily, that was brilliant.
Sheila Noisy! Fantastic!
Cecily It's a woman's world. And of all the women in it, I love you two the most. (*She holds their arms up*) Sheila and Ellen. I thank them both for the life and the love they gave me!
Sheila This is embarrassing, you silly cow.
Cecily I love you, Mum.
Sheila I love you.
Cecily Ellen, let them do their worst!
Ellen You silly cow!

Cecily tears off the bolero and throws it high in the air, turning to hug Sheila and Ellen, as the lights and sound fade back to the present. She subsides in the wheelchair and pulls the quilt over her. The drumsticks fall to the ground

Sheila And God destroyed Cecily.
Ellen They did their worst, Cecily.

Cecily emerges from the quilt

Cecily Nice day.

She smiles at them both

Ellen The sun's shining and I'm going to pick flowers. Do you want to come?
Cecily Yes.
Ellen All right.
Cecily Gary?

Ellen We'll go and find him. If he really loves me, Sheila . . .
Sheila I won't tell him.

They look at each other for a long time

Cecily Hallo, 'Len. Hallo, Mummy.
Sheila Take her to pick flowers, Ellen. Take her for the afternoon. And when you bring her home again, I'll have tea ready.

Ellen pushes Cecily out. Cecily la-las the tune of The Wizard of Oz

Dear God, why can't you let it be before . . .?
Cecily (*off*) Because, because, because, because . . .
Sheila Because, because . . .

The Lights fade to a blackout

CURTAIN

FURNITURE AND PROPERTY LIST

On stage: Wheelchair
Brightly coloured exercise balls and cubes
Paper flowers
Coloured quilt
Rubber exercise mat
Fruit bowl with bananas
Wet wipes
Other dressing at director's discretion

Off stage: Bananas (**Sheila**)
Drumsticks (**Cecily**)
Sequinned bolero (**Cecily**)

Personal: **Ellen**: handbag. *In it:* tissues, comb, lipstick, cookery book, money. Carrier bag. *In it:* brightly coloured manipulative toy

LIGHTING PLOT

Practical fittings required: nil
Interior. The same scene throughout

To open:	Full general lighting	
Cue 1	**Cecily**: **Sheila** pushes **Cecily** out *Lighting changes for flashback*	(Page 8)
Cue 2	**Cecily**: "I'm going to play my drums. See ya." *Lighting changes back to the present*	(Page 12)
Cue 3	**Sheila**: ". . . why won't you let it be before . . ." *Lighting changes to before the accident*	(Page 13)
Cue 4	**Cecily**: ". . . silly . . . silly . . . silly . . ." *Lighting changes back to the present*	(Page 14)
Cue 5	**Sheila**: "And became pregnant" *Lighting changes for flashback*	(Page 19)
Cue 6	**Ellen**: ". . . a really nice house. Sheila . . ." *Lighting returns to the present*	(Page 19)
Cue 7	**Ellen**: "Please, please don't tell him" *Lighting changes to flashback, disco lights flash on and off. Bring up spot on* **Cecily**	(Page 20)
Cue 8	**Ellen**: "You silly cow!" *Fade spot, lighting returns to the present*	(Page 20)
Cue 9	**Sheila**: "Because, because . . ." *Fade to black-out*	(Page 21)

EFFECTS PLOT

Cue 1 **Ellen**: "Please, please don't tell him." (Page 20)
Bring up disco beat music with drum solo. Increase volume, then cut. Bring up applause and cheering

Cue 2 **Ellen**: "You silly cow!" (Page 20)
Fade music and applause

MADE AND PRINTED IN GREAT BRITAIN BY
LATIMER TREND & COMPANY LTD PLYMOUTH
MADE IN ENGLAND

David's Birthday

A Play

Gillian Plowman

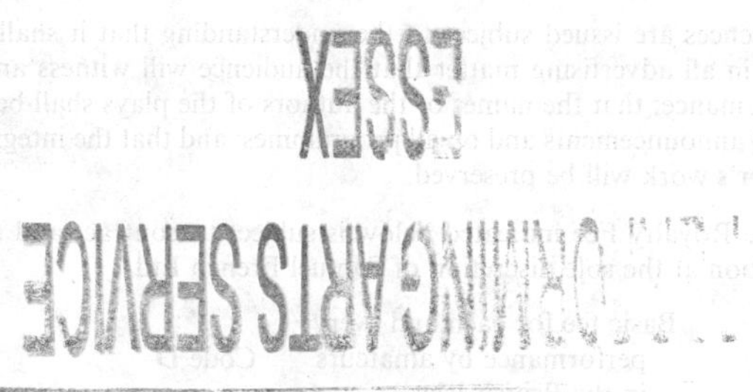

Samuel French –

New York – Sydney – To

ISBN 0 573 12062 5

DAVID'S BIRTHDAY

First performed in the 1985 All England One-Act Play Festival, with the following cast:

Maggie	Peggy Reading
Liz, her sister	Gill Plowman
John, Liz's husband	John Ritchie
Paul	Simon Allen
David, Liz and Maggie's brother	David Flint

The action takes place in Maggie's sitting room

Time—the present

FOR DAVID

DAVID'S BIRTHDAY*

Maggie's sitting-room. Afternoon

The room is comfortably furnished and includes a table, chairs and various ornaments. At the moment it is decorated with birthday cards and balloons

When the CURTAIN *rises Maggie, who is in her mid-thirties, is removing all valuable and breakable objects. After a moment the front doorbell rings*

Maggie exits and returns with her sister, Liz, and Liz's husband, John. John is carrying a bottle of wine and Liz holds a wrapped birthday present (a sweater for David)

Maggie You're bloody late.
Liz Where is he?
Maggie I've sent Paul to get him.
Liz Good old Paul.
Maggie What do you mean by that? He doesn't mind.
Liz I've sent him. I've sent him. Like he's a servant or something. Why not say "Paul's gone to get him?"
John Why not kiss your sister in a civilized manner?

John kisses Maggie but Maggie and Liz do not touch

Maggie He likes to get him.
Liz Anyway, he's not back, so we're not late.
Maggie He's got held up. You would have been late.
Liz But we're not.
Maggie You could have helped me get ready.
John What needs doing?
Maggie Nothing. It's all done.
Liz So stop making a fuss.
Maggie Now it's all done.
Liz So you had enough time.

---

*N.B. Paragraph 3 on page ii of this Acting Edition regarding photocopying and video-recording should be carefully read.

Maggie You could have helped.

John (*giving Maggie the bottle of wine*) Here you are, Maggie. Perhaps this will help.

Maggie Thanks, John. I can always rely on you, can't I? I've made jelly and blancmange and sandwiches with blackcurrant jam in. And a cake. A bloody cake.

Liz With candles on?

Maggie Yes, of course with candles on. Ten.

Liz Ten?

Maggie Ten.

John Can he count up to ten?

Liz No he can't. What did you put ten candles on for?

Maggie He can count up to ten now. You don't know. You haven't been to see him, have you? He can count really well now.

Liz It's a long way.

Maggie It's not a long way.

Liz It's further than you have to go. No, I . . . we haven't been to see him. John doesn't like to, do you?

John He's your brother.

Liz But you don't like to visit him, do you?

John No, I don't.

Liz It's too far for us.

Maggie It's only nine hundred miles from Land's End to John o'Groats for Christ's sake. Once a year, that's all you can manage. And then you come here. Why has it always got to be here?

Liz You know why that is, Maggie. Because of the kids.

Maggie You never even make the cake.

Liz You know how he likes it. I'll make it next year if you like.

Maggie Yes, fine. You make it next year.

Liz I will.

Maggie And you can make the jelly and blancmange too, and the blackcurrant jam sandwiches.

Liz Don't be ridiculous, Maggie. We can't bring all that.

Maggie You won't need to bring it—we'll come to you next year. There's no reason why not, is there? The kids aren't kids any more, are they?

John It's convenient here. Near enough to get him just for the day. And near enough for us to come. If you come to us, well, how would we get him?

Maggie In your car. You drive to David's Home, and you put him in it and you drive to your house. Then you get him out of it. It's easy. It's very simple. He's no trouble really, if you move everything out of the way—ornaments, pictures, photographs, because he loves to touch and always breaks, and you have to remember to put newspaper down in the toilet because he always misses. No, no, that's not true, you don't have to do all that. He's fine. He's really OK now. You'll see. You haven't seen him for a year. He's fine now. Marvellous really. Paul's gone to get him. You'll see. And I've put ten candles on the cake.

Liz That's good, Maggie.

Maggie Yes. He's really OK now.

Maggie exits

Liz She doesn't have to go and see him. It's no good her trying to make me feel guilty. I know I don't go. That's my choice. If she goes, that's her choice. No one makes her.

John Her conscience makes her.

Liz Don't you think I've got a conscience?

John You? We were talking about Maggie.

Liz Well talk about me. I have a conscience. I care. I just have other commitments. Maggie doesn't have children. She doesn't know what that's like. The demands all the time. She doesn't even have a husband.

John She has Paul. It's the same thing.

Liz It's not the same thing. She's not committed to Paul. She can get up and get out any time she likes.

John And so could you.

Liz You know very well I can't. I couldn't leave the kids.

John But you could leave me.

Liz I didn't mean that. You could go. But you don't need to, do you? You do all the things you want to do.

John You've made the kids your excuse for everything you haven't done.

Liz They're the reason I haven't done anything.

John If you want . . .

Liz Haven't I been a good mother, John? Talk to me. Tell me.

John I just wish . . .

Liz What?

John Yes, you've been a good mother.

Liz And a good wife. Everything's always been all right between us, hasn't it? We'll make love tonight. When we're home again. Would you like that? I've never denied you, have I?

John No.

Liz So what do you wish? John?

John That you would just do something wrong. Something not ever right.

Liz But I have, surely? I haven't been to see David. That's wrong. I know that's wrong. But there's never the time somehow. And . . . it's just awful seeing them all. David's all right. I mean, we're used to David, aren't we? It's all the others. I don't know what to do when I'm there. So that's wrong, you see. I've done something wrong. Have you, John? Have you?

John What?

Liz You've done something wrong, haven't you? What is it?

John I've never done anything, Liz. I've never done anything.

Maggie enters with a box of toys, including a red car and a packet of balloons

A car is heard drawing up outside

Maggie There's Paul's car. Blow these up. (*She hands the balloons to John*)

Maggie exits

John blows up a balloon. Liz takes off her brooch and uses the pin to burst the balloon

John turns and exits

Liz I've burst all your bubbles, haven't I?

Liz picks up a balloon and turns her back to the Audience while the Lights dim for the flashback sequence. As the Lights come up again Liz turns round. She is herself as a young girl

(*Chanting*) Rain, rain, go away,
Come on David's birthday . . .

Maggie enters, as herself when young

Maggie Daddy says you have to sit next to David at tea today.

Liz It's always me, just 'cos I'm the eldest.

Maggie It's not always you. We take it in turns.

Liz And it's your turn.

Maggie But I washed his hair last night and you know how difficult that is. Those shampoos that don't sting your eyes always sting David's eyes. He was screaming his head off and we both got soaked.

Liz I put him on the toilet twice on Sunday.

Maggie And I had to hold his hand all the time Aunt Evelyn was here so he wouldn't . . . you know . . .

Liz He ought to be put away where the dirty boys go.

Maggie Daddy smacks him when he does that but he can't smack him when Aunt Evelyn's here.

John enters, as Father

John Don't you tell anyone about that. Only we three know about that. Just the three of us. I don't smack him hard. I chastise him. He has to learn, like any other child. Don't you ever go round saying I smack my son. That's a family matter. Do you hear, child?

Maggie Yes, Daddy.

John And you?

Liz Yes, Daddy.

John You are my daughters. Each other's sister. What must you do?

Maggie
Liz } (*together*) Love each other.

They execute some sort of ritual embrace drummed into them by Father since early childhood

John And what else?

Maggie
Liz } (*together*) Love our brother as ourselves.

John And how will you do that?

Maggie Look after him always.

Liz And never send him away

Maggie
Liz } (*together*) For ever and ever, Amen.

John Your mother died giving birth to her son. She left him with us. She left us with him.

Pause. The Lights change. They revert to themselves in the present

Maggie Here they are. (*She turns towards the door*)
Liz John, where's his present?

Paul and David enter. Paul is in his thirties and lives with Maggie. David is mentally retarded and is aged thirty-two. He holds Paul's hand as a child would, clinging on in his excitement and nervousness

Everyone sings "Happy Birthday"

Maggie Happy birthday, David. (*She kisses David*)
David Happy birthday, Maggie.
Maggie No, it's your birthday. You're thirty-two.
David Thirty-two. Yes, I'm thirty-two. (*He tells Paul*) I'm thirty-two. (*He takes Paul's hand*)
Liz Happy birthday, David.
David Happy birthday, Lizzie.

David and Liz kiss

Liz You remembered my name.
David You're my sister, Lizzie.
Liz Oh, David. (*She is overcome and hugs him to her*)
Maggie You see, he's much better, isn't he?
David Don't cry, Lizzie. It's your birthday.
Liz No, David. It's yours. Look, John and I have a present for you.
David John?
Liz My husband, David. You remember John.
David Happy birthday, John.
John Happy birthday, David.

David kisses John carefully

Liz I wish he wouldn't do that.
Maggie It's only like kissing a child.
Paul It isn't though, is it?

Pause

Maggie Open your present, David.

David opens his present. It is a blue sweater

David It's nice. Red.
John It's blue.
David Yes. Blue. It's nice. Paul brought me in a nice car. Blue. (*He takes Paul's hand*)
Paul It's a grey car, David.
David Paul brought me in a grey car. What's a grey car?
Paul The car I brought you in is a grey car.
David Oh. There's my car. Grey?
Maggie It's a sodding red car.
Paul Shut up, Maggie.
John He's doing well.
David Sodding red car.
Paul Do you want to try your sweater on, David? Take the other one off.

David stands with his hands in the air and stares at Paul intently as Paul takes the sweater off. Paul is disconcerted and moves away with the sweater

Paul exits

The Lights dim for the flashback sequence. Liz and Maggie become young girls again

Maggie
Liz } (*together*) Rain, rain go away,
Come on David's birthday . . .

John becomes Father and goes to help David dress. The girls lie on their stomachs, with their feet in the air, playing a game of draughts

Liz Let him do it himself, Daddy.
Maggie He's got to learn to dress himself some time.
Liz Otherwise he'll look stupid when he's grown up. Not able to dress himself.

John exits

David tries to put the sweater on. He gets into a mess and becomes frustrated, shouting and stamping. The girls play on. David gets the red car and, with one arm in the sweater and one out, he pushes the car through their game

Liz David, get out! That was there! (*She pushes David away*)

Maggie It wasn't.
Liz It was. I was just going to take it. And that one. I would have won!
Maggie You're a liar! That wasn't there.

David pushes the car through their game again

Oh you stupid, idiotic, infantile idiot!
Liz Backward, mentally deficient, borderline brother! I hate you!
Maggie Hate you!
Liz Hate you!
Maggie Hate you!

They hit David

John enters and smacks the girls across the face

Silence

Maggie Sorry, Daddy.
John Liz?
Liz It's him who should be sorry. Say sorry, David. Sorry. Why don't you speak. Go on, speak. Say sorry, sorry, sorry! (*She shakes David*) Won't you ever speak. (*She pushes him over*)
John Liz!
Liz Sorry, Daddy.
John What must you do?

Maggie and Liz perform the ritual embrace. They pick up the game, put it away and sit in the corner with books. John helps David with the sweater

What will you be, eh? What will you do with your life? Torture me forever? Your hands are dirty. We must wash your hands. Hands are useful things, David. Use your hands and you could be a painter, or a carpenter. You could be a soldier, David. (*He puts David straight and swings his arms*)

David laughs

Or a clerk, who writes. Or a writer. You need things inside your head to be a writer. Are there things inside your head? Are you hiding things from me? Tell me, son. She did this to me. Just because—not JUST because—BECAUSE I wanted to go away you see. Leave them. I had other things to do . . . No. There was someone else. I'd saved enough money—she would have had enough to look after herself and the girls. But she wouldn't let me go. "I bear another child", she told me as I packed my case. I didn't believe her. "Your child, here, inside me". I said she was lying; she spat in my face. I struck out—she fell. . . I stayed with her till you were born, David, and then she died. She left me. Now—I can't leave you. Damn you. What can you ever be?

The Lights change and they revert to themselves, now

Liz That looks fine, John. Fits him. I think he's put on weight, though.

Maggie He likes to eat.

Liz Always did.

Maggie He doesn't get much exercise at the Home.

John He ought to. They ought to give them plenty of exercise.

David I have a nice blue sweater.

Maggie You see. Two adjectives. Bloody marvellous.

David Bloody marvellous.

Liz Maggie, can't you watch your language.

Maggie You're bloody marvellous, kid. Come on.

Maggie, David and Liz play with the balloon during the following

Maggie We're going to have tea, David.

Liz Jelly and blancmange.

Maggie Sandwiches with blackcurrant jam.

Liz And a birthday cake.

Paul enters carrying a plastic Christmas cloth

Maggie Paul, put the cloth on the table.

Paul It's plastic.

Maggie I know it's plastic.

Paul It's a Christmas cloth.

Maggie It's the only plastic cloth we've got.

David It's nice, Christmas. *Away In A Manger.*

Liz Sing it David. Can you sing it?

David sings a verse with simple actions. It is very moving. David has a lovely voice. Maggie and Liz clasp hands briefly as they listen to

David. John pours out some wine and gives both Liz and Maggie a glass

John Here's looking at you, sunshine.
Paul To you, David.

David pops a balloon and giggles. Liz and Maggie relax

Maggie Come on, Liz. Give me a hand in the kitchen.

Liz and Maggie exit

David goes to Paul and pops a balloon

Paul Don't do that.

David pops another balloon

Paul Don't DO that. (*He drains his glass*)
David Can I drink, please?
Paul Can he?
John Why not?

John gives David a glass of wine. David bites the glass, chokes and cries

Oh Christ, the idiot!
Paul It's all right. It doesn't hurt.
John I'll get him some water.

John exits

Paul Don't cry, David. (*He puts his arm round David and kisses him*)

Paul crosses the room and picks up the wine bottle. The Lights dim for the flashback sequence

John enters

Paul and John are both young bullies now. David is young, too, and holds a toy rabbit

John 'Ere, Steve, where did ya get it?
Paul Nicked it.
John Yeh? (*He snatches the bottle and drinks*) Where did ya nick it from?

Paul Bloody supermarket, didn't I. 'Elped this old girl wiv 'er trolley. 'Em all finkin' the youth of today ain't as bad as they're made out, an' I slips it in 'er trolley and no one notices a bleedin' fing. 'Allo, 'allo, there's dumbo David out on 'is own. Where's 'is old man?
John 'E's run away. You run away, sissy? Perhaps 'e's lookin' for a good time.

They push David to and fro. David grunts

Paul 'Allo, sissy. You want some fun?
John Cigarettes and whisky and wild, wild women?
Paul Give us a fag.
John Sod off.
Paul Give us a fag.

John gives him one and Paul lights it. They put it in David's mouth. He tries to puff to please them but coughs. They slap him on the back

Give 'im a drink.

They force David to drink the wine. David drops his rabbit

Hey look what I've found. It's a bunny rabbit. Your bunny is it, sissy?

They run away and taunt him with it. David falls down

John Hey, sissy, get up.

Every time David tries to get up, they knee him or knock him down

Paul I know what he needs.
John What?
Paul Jenny Maxwell.
John D'yer fink she would?
Paul Yeh, she would, for a fag.
John 'E's just 'ad me last one.
Paul You 'ad Jenny Maxwell?
John Yeh. You?
Paul Yeh.
John Bet you 'aven't.
Paul I 'ave.
John Where?

Paul Cricket pavilion.

John Bloody 'ell. Bit public innit?

Paul Yeah! Got a cheer from the lads when I'd finished. Where d'you then?

John 'Er 'ouse. 'Er mum and dad was in the front room watchin' telly at the time.

Maggie enters as Jenny Maxwell

Maggie Yeh, I don't mind. But I want a fag off each of yer.

Paul Termorrer.

Maggie And don't ya bleedin' forget. (*She sees the rabbit*) What's that?

Paul 'Is.

Maggie 'Is what?

John That's 'is little bunny rabbit, innit sissy?

Maggie Blimey. It's nice, innit? This yours, dear? Want it back? Ah, it's all soft and furry. (*She rubs it against her face*) Kiss me, David, and you can 'ave your bunny back.

David goes to kiss her but she grabs him and starts to make love to him

John Go on, give 'er one, sissy.

Maggie 'E's no sissy. 'E's a big boy, aren't you, David?

Paul Boom, boom, boom . . .

John Boom, boom, boom . . .

Just as the scene becomes unbearably gross, Liz appears

Liz David!

John Bloody 'ell. It's big sister. Scarper!

John, Paul and Maggie run off

David sinks to his knees. Liz runs to him

Liz Leave him alone. David. Oh David . . . what were they doing to you?

David Lizzie. (*He hugs her round the waist. He is crying*)

Liz The sods. (*She is crying*)

David Lizzie.

Liz I wish Mummy was here. But there's only you and me and Daddy and Mag. If she was here, she'd know what to do with you.

The Lights change. They revert to themselves now

Maggie enters with a tray holding the party food

Maggie What's the matter with him?
Liz They've given him some wine, the goons. (*She raises David to his feet and wipes his mouth*)

Paul enters with the cake and puts it on the table

Maggie Paul, you ought to know better.
Paul Sorry.

John enters with a plastic tumbler of water

John I've brought him some water. Plastic cup.
Liz Here you are, David, drink this.

David drinks

Go to the toilet now, David, and wash your hands. Can you do that?
David Yes.
Liz Go on then.
David (*moving to take Paul's hand*) You come.
Paul I'll go with him if you like.
Maggie He can manage. Anyway, I've got newspaper down in the toilet. Go on, David, go to the toilet.

David starts to undo his zip

Wait until you get there. It's rude.
David David's rude.

Maggie and Liz laugh

Liz Remember Reverend Perry?
Paul Don't laugh at him. He can't help it.
Maggie We know. We were just remembering Sunday School.
Liz Reverend Perry used to conduct us as though we were in the Albert Hall.
Maggie We had to take David. I don't think he ever understood any of it.
Liz He loved *Jesus Died For All The Children.*

The Lights dim for the flashback sequence. Liz and Maggie sit crossed-legged on the floor. David gets a tambourine from the box and marches around thumping it. Paul watches from the side. They all sing, John conducting as the Reverend Perry

Liz
Maggie } (*singing together*) Jesus died for all the children
All the children of the world
Red and yellow, black and white
All the precious in his sight
Jesus died for all the children of the world.

John Excellent, children. God in his heaven is pleased with you.

Maggie Reverend Perry, are you sure that God loves David as well.

John I'm sure, Maggie. He's near enough to see and love him. And just far enough away not to smell him. Come along, son. To the little room at the back.

Liz and Maggie snort with laughter as John takes David out

The Lights change. They revert to themselves in the present

Liz moves to light the cake candles, standing with her back to the audience. Paul stops Maggie laughing

Paul Why do you laugh at him?

Maggie So that I don't cry.

Paul There are worse things in life than being like David, you know.

Maggie Like what?

Paul He doesn't know what he's like, does he? He's daft but he doesn't know it so it doesn't matter.

Maggie It matters to me. It's mattered to me since the day he was born. And Liz . . .

Paul And nothing else has mattered. You and her and him. The only problem. The eternal triangle. It shifts and changes its angles but always keeps everyone else out. I am desperate, Maggie. I am torn apart. I am waiting for you to see me. To ask me what's the matter. To help me. But you don't see.

Maggie Yes I do.

Pause

Paul Then help me.
Maggie I can't.
Paul Ask me what's wrong.
Maggie I know what's wrong. You want David, don't you?

Pause

Paul He'll never understand.
Maggie I'm the nearest you'll get to him. Love me. Want me.
Paul I do, but you keep me out.

David enters with his zip undone

Liz Do up your zip, David.
David (*counting the candles*) One—two—three—four—five—six—seven—eight—nine—ten
Maggie See—see?
David Eleven—twelve—thirteen—fifteen—fourteen—eighteen—nineteen (*with great effort*) Twenty!

John enters

Liz John! John! He can count up to twenty!

David continues counting with great effort and excitement

David Twenty-one—twenty-two—twenty-three—twenty-four—twenty-five—twenty-six—twenty-seven—twenty-eight—twenty-nine . . .

He forgets what comes next

Liz Thirty.
David (*shouting with anger because he forgot*) Thirty! Thirty-one. Thirty-two. I'm thirty-two. I'm thirty-two!
Maggie What comes next, David?

He has forgotten, sits down and eats blancmange, spilling some

John Who taught you to count, David?
David Ann.
Liz Who's Ann?
David My teacher.
Liz (*looking at Maggie*) Have you met her?
Maggie Yes. Last time we went. She said he could count up to ten.

David She says I can have a job and live in the world.

Pause

Liz Who the bloody hell does she think she is, filling his head with rubbish.

Paul The fact that she can fill his head is something.

Liz I'm his next of kin. They've never said anything to me about him leaving the home.

Maggie They might have done if you'd taken the trouble to go there.

Liz They should have written.

Maggie You should have gone.

John What sort of a job could he do?

David Ask me. I can do a job. Ask David.

John What sort of job can you do, David?

David Gardening. I can grow things. I'm very good at gardening.

Maggie And where will you live?

David With you.

Maggie Me?

David You. (*He looks at them all*)

Liz We don't all live together.

David Oh. (*He eats some more*)

Liz They don't expect us to take him in do they? John and I can't do that.

Paul They never said anything about him leaving the Home. They only said we could keep him tonight if we want to. Only to let them know. We could, couldn't we?

Maggie And he could sleep with you, I suppose.

Liz Maggie, don't be ridiculous.

David I can sleep with Father.

Liz That's John, David. You can't sleep with John. I sleep with John.

John That was unnecessary.

Liz Do you want him to live with us?

John He's your brother.

Liz Stop saying that. It's our life. We have our children. I left David, sent him away . . . loved you.

John No, you never did. You never loved, laughed, raged, cried or faltered. Not for me. You were nothing after you left David. You never needed me. Perhaps YOU want him back.

David (*still eating*) I'll sleep with Ann.

Liz So that you can move out.

David I'll sleep with Ann.

Liz (*to David*) Then you'd better bloody well stay where you are then.

Maggie He could come to us sometimes.

Paul No, Maggie, no.

Maggie I thought that's what you'd want. There are plenty of gardens round here he can dig in. Or do you think he would come between us? He wouldn't, you know. We'd have our own eternal triangle. I love you, you love David, David loves me, and then we'd all turn over and I love David, and David loves you and you love me . . . (*She keeps repeating this*)

Paul Maggie, stop!

Liz David, I didn't mean it. We'll never send you away. Never. We promised Daddy . . .

Maggie To love each other . . .

Liz And love our brother as ourselves . . .

Maggie And look after him always . . .

Liz And never send him away . . .

Maggie
Liz } (*together*) For ever and ever, Amen.

David comes to them, quietly singing "Ring a ring o' roses", Liz, Maggie and David join hands and sing the nursery rhyme over and over, faster and louder as they go round in circles John and Paul circle round them calling

Paul Maggie! Stop! Let me in! Maggie! Maggie!

John I wanted you to love me, Liz. It's too late. It was always too late! Liz! Liz!

As they reach the climax of the rhyme—All fall down—they let go hands and Maggie falls on Paul and Liz on John as they crumble to the floor

Silence. David pushes the car

David Sodding red car. Happy birthday, David. (*He blows out the candles*)

Black-out

CURTAIN

FURNITURE AND PROPERTY LIST

On stage: Table
Chairs
Ornaments
Birthday cards
Balloons
Glasses

Off stage: Bottle of wine (**John**)
Blue sweater—gift wrapped (**Liz**)
Box of toys including a red car, a tambourine, a packet of balloons, a game of draughts, books, toy rabbit **(Maggie)**
Plastic Christmas cloth **(Paul)**
Tray. *On it:* party food—jelly, blancmange, blackcurrant jam sandwiches, plates, dishes and cutlery **(Maggie)**
Birthday cake with ten candles, matches **(Paul)**
Plastic tumbler of water **(John)**

Personal: **Liz:** brooch, handkerchief
Paul: cigarettes and lighter in his pocket

LIGHTING PLOT

Interior. The same scene throughout

To open: General lighting

Cue 1 As **Liz** turns her back to the audience (Page 4)
Lights dim for flashback sequence

Cue 2 **John:** "She left us with him." (Page 5)
Pause. Lights up

Cue 3 **Paul** moves away with the sweater (Page 7)
Lights dim for flashback sequence

Cue 4 **John:** "What can you ever be?" (Page 9)
Lights up

Cue 5 **Paul** picks up the wine bottle (Page 10)
Lights dim for flashback sequence

Cue 6 **Liz:** ". . . she'd know what to do with you." (Page 13)
Lights up

Cue 7 **Liz:** "He loved *Jesus Died For All The Children*." (Page 14)
Lights dim for flashback sequence

Cue 8 **John** takes **David** out (Page 14)
Lights up

Cue 9 **David** blows out the candles (Page 18)
Black-out

EFFECTS PLOT

Cue 1 As **Maggie** removes the breakable objects (Page 1)
Front doorbell

Cue 2 As **Maggie** enters with a box of toys (Page 4)
Car draws up

MADE AND PRINTED IN GREAT BRITAIN BY
LATIMER TREND & COMPANY LTD, PLYMOUTH
MADE IN ENGLAND